paper wings

paper wings

Sarah Tassin

ACKNOWLEDGEMENTS

Thank you, mom and dad, for supporting me in every journey I take.

to the lovers and the dreamers and the fighters of the world

darling i'm a mess

poetry is like a river
it ebbs and flows in a million different directions
but each carefully crafted and beautifully made
it's alive with color and sound and schools of fish eager to swim
like emotions flowing through your veins

and when all is said and done
if you ever fall off the edge
the river will be there to catch you
and float you right back to shore

i hate you or i love you
choose your weapon

i've always preferred vanilla to chocolate
call me bland or plain crazy
but i live a life made of chocolate
full of sweet goodbyes and rich beginnings
and sometimes it's overwhelming enough
that i crave the simplicity
of a vanilla candle and a lazy day in bed

-vanilla

we bloomed on a sleeping mountaintop
until what was once dormant
shook beneath us
and roared awake

-our fault (line)

loving someone is the bravest thing you can do

if i could capture starlight
i'd put it safely in a jar
and study it's silken rays
i'd watch it bounce off the walls
and reflect through my wondering eyes

maybe then i'd understand the craftsmanship
that pieced together our daunting world

-starlight in a jar

please forgive me for the things i do before i find you

my mind is a fortress of solitude

i might feel everything
and you might not feel much at all
but at least i have the decency
to know the difference between right and wrong

-the difference between you and i

the safest you'll ever feel
is when you drift off in someone's arms
and they're still there when you wake

i'm a bit obsessed with the idea of an eternity with you

the universe is infinite
a black canvas frosted with planets and ecosystems and
intention
the milky way churns defiantly
and the stars glitter the sky with wonder
the universe is devastatingly beautiful
she bewitches all who dare to peek
everything has its place
even we have a purpose among the galaxy
even our very souls are made of stardust
because in spite of it all
we too are infinite

i want you so badly
i would tear apart a city brick by brick to find you
but i have to let it eat me up inside instead
because you've made it clear you don't want to be found

-one sided love

God called out your name
and wrote you into the stars
He died so that you could live
the least you could do
is believe He exists

my heart is an empty canvas
so paint it with your words

i would've walked through hell for you

you don't know me like you used to
you beat me
and tortured me
but i've had time to heal
and now you wouldn't even recognize me

i swam in your love
like it was a pool of diamonds
and i had the rare privilege to dive in

she grew vines down her arms where wildflowers used to grow
and replaced the stars in her eyes with gaping black holes
but i couldn't sit by and watch as her reflection turned to stone
so i split my heart in two and gave her a piece of my soul

you are enough
you are so enough
it is unbelievable how enough you are

-i was once told

i need you to hear me when i say
i'm so sorry
because i mean it with all that i am
i was still growing
and you were collateral
i came out stronger
but i'll never forget or forgive
what i did to you to survive

he was made of pure gold
but she was coated in silver
and the two weren't meant to cross paths

-coated in silver

what happens when the responsible one
is no longer responsible for what happens?

i'll admit to being a lot at fault
i wasn't the easiest pill to swallow
but i was never a bitter taste of salt
and you were wrong to assume i'm hollow

-i felt it all

i'm obsessed with finding an always
but no one seems to want my forever

-always&forever

romeo and juliet
don't even come close
new and crazy met
and young love spoke

i remember my past but i don't think i lived it
it's like looking through glass
is that really me?

i think i can put the pieces together
but God i don't know
if i even should

i fit into all the puzzles
by breaking what i promise
by redefining my edges
by rebuilding who i am
by losing my sanity

and i kinda love it
if i'm really being honest

i fought until i couldn't recognize the difference between the
pain and the peace

if you died today
if you died this second
and you had one last wish
would you waste it?

you left me
traded me in like an old bedside table
beaten and bruised with the markings of old coffee rings
and stained with memories unworthy of keeping

we made a scrapbook full of twisted memories

don't fall for the butterflies
they're a warning sign

i deserve better than you

she told me i could trust her
and that i was her best friend
all while her fingers were crossed behind her back
and i believed it without hesitation

but now i check for both hands
before i give it all away

-toxic friendships

just because you pick me up
doesn't mean you'll drive me home
don't assume i'll be waiting
when there are 10 other guys
holding their doors open

-fight for me

they say trust is what floats a relationship
so to my knowledge we were drowning

i use coined phrases and stolen looks to hide in plain sight
because the perfect disguise
is to be seen
but never noticed

the biggest parts of me
are usually the things
no one even knows
i went through

that first slice of wedding cake
when he takes your hand
and you do it together
that's the start of forever

oh tell me you understand

you know the funny thing about bandages
they do a great job at covering
but they'll never be able to actually fix what's broken
that's up to you

just because they let you go
doesn't mean you're not holding on for dear life
just because they're gone
doesn't mean you're free

i'll spend my whole life wondering
if the next hit i take
is gonna be the one to knock me down

-anxiety

if i bleed and no one sees
how will they know
what it took to get here?

a daughter needs a mother
like a flower needs the sun
a sound compass to guide us
and a tether to bring us back

i won't even burden you with the knowledge
that all it takes is one word from you
to save me from drowning alone

the rain lingers after a storm
even if only in sprinkles
just because i've stopped sobbing
doesn't mean i won't give in to the tears
every once in a while

we spend our lives searching
we make it our whole purpose
change and want
there's no such thing as being content
it's human nature to always want more
and it'll be the death of us

don't tease me with questions that need answering
you know i can't help but probe
until every stone has been turned

don't you dare start to judge
you made me this way
i was still laid out drying
when you molded a new shape

you can't cancel someone
just because you say so
you can't pick and choose
like the hand of God
because if we're being honest
and you were on the chopping block

you'd all be canceled

-cancel culture

if it tastes bitter
wouldn't you spit it out?

then why do we keep chewing
the lies and hate we're being fed?
(with a smile nonetheless)

there was a fire in my house
burning all of me away
you could smell the growing smoke
and yet you left me to decay

who gave society reign over you?

i don't talk to my best friends anymore
or
actually
they don't talk to me
and it's never really bothered me before
at least that's what i tell myself
to hide the fact
that everyone has moved on
so i guess that i should too

you're proving their point for them

you stood up for what was right
so they cut you at your waist
you hurdled every obstacle
so they built them up higher

they have you cornered

what's your next move?

watch me shatter under the pressure of your embrace

i wonder if that old stone path
connecting 2 simple houses in south louisiana
knows it once held the innocent pitter patter
of my little feet?

i just realized that heartbreak
is like when you've been drinking a latte
and you get to the bottom
where only black coffee remains

that bitter taste left in your mouth stings
but will slowly fade with every sip you take

i promise to never tire of the way you say my name

you were the love of my life
but i was never yours

i think i knew that deep down
but i was too afraid of losing the one constant i've ever known

you didn't mean to hurt me
i think you even loved me in your own way

but now you have the chance to have the love you wanted
and this is the part
where i step out of the way

-the valerie to your stefan

the moment you have to walk away
and glance one last time
at the person you'll never see again
that's the moment you notice how privileged you are
to stare into their eyes

you feel like you're losing it all
when you let your grip go
but your hands are only empty
until you find your permanent home

-finding

i thought i had failed
when i finally stopped swimming and started to drown
but little did i know
that the moment you start to hold your breath
your survival instinct kicks in
and you find your reason
to fight again

-fighting

i was teetering on the edge
walking a slipping tight rope
and all i could do was close my eyes

but then i saw you
step right beside me
and hold out your hand

i grabbed you so tightly
and smiled so wide
just as you pushed me
and i fell to my demise

-falling

i get to call you mine
and hold your hand
whenever i want
whenever i can

i get to watch you
learn and grow
and be there
every step of the way

i get to know
what makes you tick
and study your eyes
until they finally close

-i get to love you

i think i know who stares back at me when the eyes meeting my gaze aren't my own

death has no hold on me
because i am not afraid

yes i'm afraid of dying
but i'm not afraid
that death is the end

i've been holding my breath for years
and i didn't even notice
the monitor has been flashing red
and even though
it's time to come back
pretty please don't pinch me yet

i can't promise you that i'll be here when you get ready
not because i want to move on
but because maybe i need to

watch the world burn
with your hands tied behind your back
and then try to convince me
that everything is okay

i was tossed aside
once i was empty
once you had used up
every part of me

i couldn't smile anymore
or make you laugh
or take your side
when someone made you mad

so you tossed me aside
like you never even knew me

-garbage

there's something about the nostalgia
of childhood summers
that whenever i get sad now
i go on a drive somewhere sunny
blast country music
sip on sweet iced tea
and i'm all good

you said don't let it get to my head
so it pierced my heart instead

toxic means something different to each person
to me
dairy is toxic
even though it may not be for you
if she says your toxic

you are

within a split second
our childhood was over

and we never even got to say…

-goodbye

time kept going
but i fought to slow down

i am not afraid of you
you who stares back at me
waiting for me to break
you who were there after every step
to make sure that i fell
whom i called 'me'
because myself was nowhere to be found

i am not afraid of you
i found the cage where i was hiding
and locked you there instead
you scream and laugh
day and night
'the little voice in my head'
pounding headaches
mimic the struggle to rein you in

i am not afraid of you
i will not give in
and let back out the monster
that played the role i was supposed to fill
for 5 years of my life

i gave it my all and it gave me my scars

i am a stunning cherry blossom tree
but you look at me and wish
i was a field of swaying bluebonnets
instead

the fits of color in a single breath of sky
are enough to fill a whole world
and create a new one to sit at its side

-the detail in a sunrise

when i watch the rain play on the edge of my window
i wonder how many drops have the privilege of dancing atop
your golden skin

i was taught not to need a man
i was taught to be content
but i was raised on superman
and i want my clark kent

shed your tears like they're made of pure gold
and don't apologize for having the courage
to break the wall between heart and mind

all i need
is a cherry ring pop
and the promise of forever

i lost myself to the bogs of sight
when there were six other senses

dance with me
when the rain pours
my best friend
is all i'm looking for
teach me love
and i'll learn grace
watch me grow with all we face

grab my hand
and i'll grab onto yours
what you give me
i promise to give more
you say always
and i'll say forever

if we bruise
we won't break
because i'll fight until i lose
just ignore all the hate
and please choose me

just choose me

all i've got
is my name and my heart
not a lot
but enough to give us a real shot
i'll be here

when the rain pours

he was dripping in darkness
but tender at his core
all you had to do was take the road less traveled
to hold his beating heart

-rhysand and feyre

if you dip a rose in honey
will its beauty stick a little longer?
will the sweet mask the intolerable pain?
or will the red still fade away
and the thorns cut deep

when your heart shatters
you become obsessed with putting it back together
but what if i told you
200 growing seeds are more powerful
than one wilting flower will ever be?

-plant a new heart

i tried to swallow the truth
but it stuck like peanut butter
to the tip of my mouth
and the only way to wash it down
was with a swig of sour milk and a taste of stinging blood

i don't believe fictional romances give us false hope
but instead teach us the sacrifice and purity
true love is supposed to encompass

i'm not broken
just because my gears spin right instead of left
and i stand up when you push me down

i'm not broken
because i've traded my wings for a tail
and found a brilliant new way home

i'm not broken
you're just looking at me from the wrong angle

-the wrong angle

i'm sick and tired of feeling ugly
just because instagram tells me so
half of who i am i can't control
and the other half is who i choose to be

if you can find beauty
in both the haunting night and glowing day
you can find beauty
in me

illuminate my existence
the way pieces of starlight drip from the night sky
and guide my dreams safely home

how hard can i bite my tongue
before i draw a taste of blood?

we spend our lives searching for the gold at the end of the
rainbow
when the rainbow was the real treasure all along

she was visually appealing
like a piece of chocolate candy
dipped in plastic
and coated in lies

i'll never forget what pure ecstasy feels like

you don't need to be saved from your pain
you just need a hand to hold through it

-a hand in the fire

i'm weighing down my end of the scale
unable to lift it up to meet your gaze

with every truth comes a lie
a balance to remain intact
but i seem to have come without my due
because being yourself is not enough
to earn a seat at the table of life

i have no more to hide and no more to say

i'm sorry i failed
i'm sorry i did what i did
i'm sorry there's blood on both our hands now

but the demon in the mirror told me i had to

i just wish you were so obviously in love with me as much as i am with you

-isn't it obvious

this is a cautionary tale
of a girl who dreamed too big
they said she could never fail
until the moment that she did

she grew with wonder in her eyes
but with each passing year
the wonder in her died
until her vision was just a smear

'move on' they told her
you're just getting older
we sold you false truths
but still expect you to choose
right every time
it's not our fault that you're blind

-blind

he had tattoos on his knees
but he never hesitated to fall on them
for her

-ACOMAF

one day when my mind sends out a shock wave of ache
when a mental hand reaches so far it touches the foggy glass
behind my eyes
i'll finally be able to grab hold of you

i hope someday
my biggest flaws and worries
become his favorite parts of me

-someday

you have to understand
i couldn't fight to lose anymore

you and me are like a spoonful of honey
the pain slightly overpowers the sweet
and there's a million people we could be falling for
but i'll keep on falling
until your lips don't taste like honey
anymore

-honey

i wish love was epic
the kind where stars fall to engulf us with light
and the fabric of time rips at our command
where fire burns in the reflection of our souls
and cities vanish in our violent wake
the kind of love that has death bowing at our feet
'the end' shying away from our mighty power

because even the grave cannot conquer an epic love

i need you
but i have no right to ask you to need me back
that choice is yours to make
and yours alone

-need me

it infuriates me
that no matter how much effort i put in
you'll never even know i lifted a finger

i plan to change the world
even if it's just yours

i want my kids to have your brown hair
and my blue eyes
i want them to have your smile
and my dimples

but most of all
i want my kids to have you

you hurt me and made me think it was funny

there's an empty chair and an unused coffee mug
a salty tear in the place where a soft hand used to touch
no more them
no more 'us'
just you
and what once was

-what once was

my birthday was yesterday
i guess you forgot

at least that's what i tell myself
to mask the crippling truth
that you just didn't care

-nineteen

i fall in love with you
with every single thing that you do
i know it's not enough
but i'd give my whole world to have you
and i know you don't feel the same
but baby i'm not fighting to lose
if only you'd give me time
i'd make you learn to love me too

-learn to love me too

i can't explain it
i look into your eyes
and i just know

people make fun of me for reading
because they know if they ever did
they'd have to face the reality
that the world isn't made of sarcasm and superficiality
but poetry and purpose and passion
and the knowledge that we were meant to be more

and that scares the hell out of them

i am made of my music
the songs i choose to listen to choose who i will be today
so press shuffle
and shake the hand of each girl you meet

i wish i had more time
to become familiar with every crevice and every word
to ever exist

-know-it-all

i bet she's really short
and really thin
and really good at everything
i bet she's all i'm not
and even more that i'll never be
i bet she's anyone
as long as they aren't

me

-the girl in your dreams

i let her down
yet she didn't turn her back on me
but i believe she would have
if reflections had a say

i'm obsessed with a sad song
down a highway late at night
you broke a little bit inside
when you got home

-sad song

why is vulnerable and loyal and total love just a bedtime story
i've been read my entire life
someone come take the book out of my hands
and hold them in yours instead
someone bring my fairytales to life
and prove the whole world wrong

someone
if you're listening
please don't be just a bedtime story

- *'someone' the bedtime story*

i don't understand why i'm in so much physical pain from
something that's purely emotional

sometimes i dream that you'd walk in my room and tackle me
we'd sit for hours
you and me
in our little bubble
just like you never even left and i never even cried
and we never even slowly switched out
'i love you' for 'goodbye'

-some movie

the world is so cruel
and for what reason other than because it can be

my reflection might be whole
but don't you dare try to forget
that i am still putting the pieces together on the inside

i'm not pretty enough to be causing trouble and expecting it to
fix itself

you are the sea
you are a beautiful
never ending masterpiece
i breathe you in
and i have never felt so free
i trace along your perfectly carved edges and dare to dive in
your body is cool and powerful and full of life
i could explore and float in your presence for an eternity
your current captures me and i willingly submit with all that i
am

you are the raging sea

but the sea is a dangerous thing
new threats emerge the deeper you swim and the longer you stay
but when i try to leave
i am stuck
drowning in your undertow
(i should've known with just one taste, how bitter and
unsatisfying you really are)

-love is like the sea

kindness spreads like butter on a biscuit

if it isn't warm and sincere
it's not going anywhere

in my dreams i am in paris
i wake every morning to the cozy warmth of sunlight peeking
through my silky white curtains
i dress in fancy rompers and mutter broken french to everyone i
pass

i am perfectly free
and utterly alone
but i am not lonely
for who could be lonely in a city such as paris?

-serenity

people say
"i never knew i was drowning until i came up for air"
but as someone who felt myself sink
and went silent as my lungs filled
coming up for air couldn't give me back the sanity i lost from all
those years of water damage

-water damage

i gave all that i was to you

and then one day
you gave it all back
wrapped all of us up and set it at my door
you took one last look at me
content with the decision you had made
and walked away

i've never had the guts to open up that box
because if i did maybe i'd realize
that i helped you pack it

-placing blame

every word
every end
every choice
hits me like a brick and i watch the wall i've spent countless
hours and deep breaths and pep talks building
turn to dust at my feet
and when it does
the whole world acts like i'm the only one
who can't seem to keep anything standing
no one ever stops to think
that i've been building my wall
all while someone was on the other side
tearing it down

-internal war

it takes one heartbeat
to turn a kingdom to rubble
but it takes an entire lifetime
to build it back up
so before you tell someone to get over it
remember that some of us don't want to just leave it be

some of us want our kingdoms back

-queen of hearts

i'm afraid of being ordinary

i don't want to be just another blip on the radar that's come and
gone
i want to inspire and evolve and rattle this world
i'm not afraid of dying or of losing
i'm not afraid of the unknown
i'm afraid of waste
and i'm fearful of a ticking clock
but most of all i'm terrified that i'll never get my chance to be
extraordinary

i am going to be okay
despite the problems and consequences and suffering that today
brought
because God promises us that every day will end and night will
fall
he tattooed his promise in the sky in the form of stars
so when i'm having a tough day
i count the billions of specks above my head
and thank God for giving me tomorrow
to try again

sometimes i wish i was pretty
maybe then i'd be happy

i wanna believe in love
i wanna believe i'm worthy of it
but i keep being left
and let down
and mistreated
i give people all of me without hesitation
and yet i'm played for a fool every time
so i think it's time to give up on love
until love decides not to give up on me

i wonder all the things you show to them
that were once shown to me
how much of 'us' was never even just ours
and you now pass onto someone new

the person who i thought gave me their soul
somehow came out of this
with their soul completely intact

can you imagine the beauty within a single raindrop?

carve me open so that you may learn to understand the vast
untold secrets i hold

if i could drink red wine i would
because it reminds me of your lips
holding the glass makes me feel powerful
probably more so than it should

there once was a girl with ember eyes
and a rage that was incandescent
they tried to douse her with muttered promises
but she refused to stop and listen

when they finally held her down
and vanquished any part of her that was different
her eyes were matte and black as coals
labeled 'the one in need of forgiveness'

-fire

you used to melt in my mouth
like a piece of caramel
but now your lips are icy blue
and my fingertips sting of frostbite

i don't know when our fire became so cold
or when we traded the bold for something so pale
all I know is that i long for the days
when our love was anything but frozen

-frozen

you and me
side by side
take my hand
and we shall go
into the unknown

rose colored glasses
paint the world with harmonious reds
clouded thoughts
paint the world with stormy blues
emerald eyes
paint the world with powerful greens
and wild imaginations
paint the world with something utterly brand new

if i choose to be ignorant
i choose to stay forever in awe

for every
sight
sound
smell
taste
and touch
we encounter
there are a billion more
we may never even discover

i admire the way the wind so elegantly brushes past
never distracted
always moving
the wind whispers to us
if we dare to listen
for she knows the true purpose
we all have been searching for

i have lost myself more times than i have found my way back
does that make me a lost soul
or a soul that is simply lost?

i believe if we find love
we should cling to it with our whole being
love is powerful
but it is rare
and if you believe it is not
you have been deceived

take me with you when you go
i wish not to be left behind
it is what i am most fearful of
to be forgotten in a world that is on the brink of imploding from
within

we often forget
there is just as much beauty in an erupting volcano
as there is in a tranquil forest

i wish to be looked at with the same intensity
that fuels the starry night

i can't stand it when you complain
as if there isn't a world full of things
to be thankful for today

scores are God's way of giving us a peak into his inspiration for building this world

if you actually cared about me
you'd text first

i've been told so many times
to give up
and i've been let down enough times
that i should

i guess i can live with being ordinary
if i get to be ordinary with you

today is not the day
right now is not the time
i know
but maybe you could find the right words to say
so i won't feel so alone

i gave my heart to you
and when we were through
i didn't have the heart to ask for it back

i am made of the moments in-between

we keep repeating the same mistakes
because the world seems to thrive off of trauma

there's a subtle drop in your heart when the one you love refers
to you as "no one"

you can let go now
i'll be okay

i know who i am

and for the first time

i am not ashamed

one miniscule word
holds our whole life in its hand
'utter my name' it calls
'and I will set you free'
but instead we fall for a sweeter word
with a much sharper sting

-the freedom in saying 'no'

music is a sixth sense
it activates every other sense in its presence
with it your eyes see colors
your nose smells spices
your tongue tastes sweetness
your hands graze silk
and your ears are the window to it all

i write poems based on what i'm listening to at that very moment
and
as it turns out
i listen to a lot of love songs

remember when you were a kid
and the idea of pain
was simply a scrape on your knee

oh how we've evolved

you made a fool out of me
yet again
but
yet again
i came crawling back

it's raining outside right now
and all I can think about
is how the raindrops dance in harmony
but I have no one to dance with me

-dancing alone

all chapters end
you know that
so i shouldn't have to remind you
that there will be another
and each one has a purpose
otherwise the story is incomplete

-embrace the story you have written

the end is never really the end
it's simply a prologue to another beginning

ABOUT THE AUTHOR

Photo credit Tara Bennett, www.taraloo.com

Sarah Tassin is a writer living in Nashville, Tennessee. She is studying at Belmont University where she spends most of her free time daydreaming and making coffee runs to Dunkin Donuts. Sarah has been exploring thoughts through poetry and prose for many years now and enjoys writing about intimate and relatable topics. She hopes you find a way to connect with her writing and maybe even realize that, in spite of it all, you are not alone.

Made in the USA
Coppell, TX
21 December 2022

90430379R00114